BROKEN HEART

A One-Act Drama Presentation

By Linda (Medill) MacDonald

(AKA Linda J. MacDonald)

DURATION: Approximately 40 - 45 minutes

Eight to ten copies needed for production
(Director, Six Characters, Lighting Engineer, Sound Engineer,
Set Design, Stage Manager/Props; possibly more if use live
musicians)

H+ HEALING COUNSEL PRESS

Revised 1989
Revised 1995
Revised 2002
Newly adapted for Malibu 2004
Updated format 2022

ISBN: 979-8-9864143-0-0

Cover Art © by Deborah Gronholz

Cover art available for purchase for programs, advertising, and posters on author's website:

www.lindajmacdonald.com

Published by

H┿ HEALING COUNSEL PRESS
Gig Harbor, WA

To view an amateur video sample of a teenage production:

https://vimeo.com/372659178

Author welcomes AMAZON Reviews from anyone who has watched, played a role, or produced the play, recently or in the past.

Author email: info@lindajmacdonald.com

<u>What Others Are Saying:</u>

"I have had the privilege of experiencing *Broken Heart* since it's debut in the early 1980's. I have seen it in many different venues, with many different actors, and with various script modifications. The Spirit has consistently and mightily used Broken Heart to reveal the battle that goes on for every young person's heart. It also powerfully demonstrates Jesus' heart for us and the beauty of receiving a new and restored heart from him. I highly recommend it."

~Jeff Vancil
Former Young Life Regional Director
Western Washington
Senior Associate, Centered

"*Broken Heart* is one of those rare dramatic jewels that can both tap into our deepest sorrows while giving us a real shot at hope. I am grateful for this powerful and moving production."

~Chap Clark, PhD
author, <u>Hurt: Inside the World of Today's Teenagers</u>
Vice Provost and Professor of Youth, Family, and Culture
Fuller Theological Seminary

"With multiple themes stirring many hearts, *Broken Heart* is one of the most creative and inspiring plays I've ever seen in 40 years of ministry."

~Craig Englert,
Senior Pastor, Hope Chapel, Kihei Maui

———————

"I have watched *Broken Heart* re-enacted in front of thousands of teen-agers all over America. It is truly an inspired play that captures the miracle of the love of Jesus healing one hurting human heart of the enormous, wrenching pain caused by sin's alienation. And it is not merely one girl's story--it can be all of our stories."

~Doug Burleigh
Former President, Young Life
Associate, International Foundation, Washington, D.C.

FOREWORD

Churches can make one of two serious mistakes: One is to change the message. That should never be. There is power in preaching and teaching the old Biblical truths. That's our only hope. The other mistake is to refuse to change methods. When a church is bound by tradition it loses its relevancy. If methods didn't change over the years we wouldn't be using church buildings, pews, hymnals, organs, athletic programs, radio and hundreds of other helpful tools.

The avenue of drama is a relatively untapped tool for presenting old truths. The Drama Department of Southeast Christian Church recently performed "Broken Heart" for a Sunday morning worship service. Traditional? No. Effective? Definitely. This drama involving just five players and a narrator was absolutely the most moving and clear portrayal of the meaning of Christ's atoning sacrifice I've ever seen.

"Broken Heart" depicts a young girl growing up and experiencing difficulties and emotions that almost every person relates to. Using brief excerpts of contemporary songs that communicate people's search for meaning, a well-written narration that gives the story depth and symbols of the crucifixion that everyone understands, the drama drives home the point that Christ's death was for me. The drama makes clear that while Satan's "toys" promise pleasure, they bring pain. Only Christ can forgive and make all things new.

Over 6,000 people witnessed this drama during our Sunday morning worship service and were deeply touched by it. Over 30 came forward at the end to make a commitment to Christ.

I'm confident scores of others made quiet vows of recommitment. I would recommend "Broken Heart" to any group seeking to effectively communicate the meaning of Christ's death on the cross. It is very well done!

~Bob Russell
Senior Minister, Southeast Christian Church
Louisville, Kentucky

PREFACE

My inspiration for this drama came out of a prayer time with a close friend who was suffering from depression due to an accumulation of hurts in her life. Later, when writing a brief skit for an upcoming youth retreat, I sought to incorporate several of the lessons that came out of that prayer time together. However, my skit ideas seemed disjointed and didn't make sense. I bowed my head and asked the Lord to pull the pieces together.

Suddenly, the entire outline for the play, beginning to end, dropped into my mind. My first response? I wept, overcome by the love and power of Jesus and His work on the cross. After five minutes of uncontrolled weeping, my next response was skepticism. *No one* does plays using nails, sticks, oranges, and other such ridiculous props. Then the Lord gently reminded me of Peter, who was willing to get out of the boat, even though he had never seen anyone else (besides Jesus) do this before. He stepped out in faith, as Jesus' bidding, even though everyone else played it safe. Taking a deep breath, I too, decided to take a step into unfamiliar territory.

At the risk of looking foolish, I coached a small cast at the retreat into using the outline the Lord had given me. We recorded the production and that became the basis for the first script. When the "skit" was over, the teen audience seemed stunned into silence. Then the weeping began. Some kids even ran out the door to cry in private. I directed the cast to come alongside of some of these young people to pray with them. The Holy Spirit moved on these kids in a powerful way.

Two weeks later, my pastor asked me to put together a team to produce the play for a Sunday morning service. Again, the rudimentary script and use of the props were all the cast had to rely on. I remembered to warn the pastor to have Kleenex ready.

Again, at the end of the play, the tears began to flow. We fanned out into the congregation to pray with folks, as the spirit led. One girl from a local Young Life club told her YL leader, Tom Jonez, about the play. Since he knew me personally, he invited me to bring the cast to put it on for entertainment night at Warm Beach Camp for 300 Young Life kids, without seeing it first. I was a bit nervous doing it for such a large group for the first time.

After the play was over, the kids were instructed to have a time of solo reflection, and then head back to their cabins. The feedback from the small group cabin-times that followed was tremendous.

When the President of Young Life, Doug Burleigh, heard about the play, he had it sent up to Young Life's Malibu Club in Canada, sight unseen, to be used after the weekly "cross talk." A professional actor from Colorado, Sandy Silverthorne, did an amazing job playing "Satan." Soon, the play spread to all the Young Life summer camps in the United States as well.

The results have been far beyond my expectations, as hundreds of thousands have been touched by the play. I have received grateful letters and requests for scripts from all over the world. Based on my knowledge of Young Life's inclusion of the play at most of its camps for 15 years (longer at Wild Horse Canyon and Malibu), other youth camps, television in Europe, many churches, Christian schools, and extensive use in other situations, I estimate the play has been seen by over three million people world-wide.

This particular script for "Broken Heart" incorporates ideas I have received over the years from others who have either directed or acted in the play. In particular, I have added an optional scene with Mike, Satan, and Jesus to provide more material for *guys* to relate to. However, the problem of guys being able to relate to the play is only in the eyes of the unimaginative. While the lead character is a girl, she represents *every one* of us. In this latest version, Sally's name has been changed to "Lisa" in order to make it more contemporary. If you saw an early version of the play and are attached to the "Sally Smith" name, feel free to alter your master copy of the script to change her name back to "Sally" again.

While the play is simple, it can be expanded through the use of slides during the songs, or by using live musicians. From the first performance at a small youth retreat up to the present, I have encouraged groups to be creative and adapt the script according to their audiences and the talents of the cast members. I support Directors who wish to update the music, incorporate dance or mime, and use costumes to fit their needs, as long as the basic message is left intact.

I recommend making good use of music during the play, without cutting the clips too short. The audience is hearing all of this for the very first time and will enjoy the musical interludes, even though a person familiar with the play may tire of them.

Finally, my preference is that the play continues to be performed in nonprofit/free settings. However, please keep in mind that when using copyrighted, secular songs, licensing will likely be needed regardless of if tickets are sold.

~Linda J. MacDonald (formerly Medill)

ACKNOWLEDGEMENTS

While the contributors to the play are too numerous to name, I must list a few. Sharon Stevens played the first Narrator and invented some of the best lines in the play. Roger Higdon played one of the early "Satan" figures and added many of Satan's lines which I incorporated into the script. In the early days, Kevin Stevens often played "Jesus" and did a superb job projecting just the right warmth and smiles that you'd want from Jesus in this sensitive role. Ron DeMiglio played "Mike" (earlier known as "Macho Mike") which got a rise out of the audience in his leather jacket (popular at the time), and sudden appearance from the midst of the crowd. He added just the right interpretation for this character.

I am grateful for the help of my friend, Pam Gillet, who has directed the play many times at both Malibu and Washington Family Ranch's Wild Horse Canyon. Her suggestions have been pivotal to the evolution of the play. I also want to thank Bill McGhee, Moe Girard, Michelle Robertson, and the Malibu Summer Staff Interns for their contributions. I appreciated the prayer support and guidance that Gail Grimston provided when she oversaw so many productions of the play at Malibu. And, finally, I want to salute Heidi Holly for passing along her script suggestions from the 2004 production at Malibu.

I wish I could name all of the people who worked so hard to project the true meaning of Jesus' work on the cross through this play. Lighting persons, sound engineers, plus actors and directors, all did their best to help folks find its healing application to our lives. Hugs to all of you!

CONTENTS

<u>CAST OF CHARACTERS</u>

(In Order of Appearance)

NARRATOR - A person who reads with expression and enthusiasm.

LISA SMITH - A sensitive but vibrant girl who, as a victim of divorce. Portrays her inner feelings from ages 5 to 18. Wears pigtails or braids when young.

MRS. SMITH - Lisa's mother. Wears an apron.

SATAN - The sly villain who deceives Lisa into thinking he is her only true friend. Some productions have him wearing a black cape.

JESUS - A strong but gentle Savior with warm eyes and a commanding stance.

MIKE - A handsome, romantic, confused teenage boy.

CREW – Director, Stage Manager (Set Design, Props), Lighting Director, Music/Sound Director.

PROPS (In order)

LISA'S BENCH - A piano bench works well

HEART - A large orange (need two that are same shape & size, one already covered in foil)

TWIG OF BITTERNESS - A large twig from a tree or bush

NAIL OF ANGER

NAIL OF JEALOUSY } Three huge 5–6 inch nails (railroad

NAIL OF ILLICIT SEX spikes work well)

NEGATIVE GLASSES – Green-lens sunglasses. Some use Giant sunglasses for effect.

OLD-STYLE BRIEFCASE - (like a doctor's bag) containing:

>   *Light Day Pack
>   *Several $20 bills
>   *Bottle of beer & bottle of pills
>   *Playboy Magazine cover (with another magazine inside) and a package of condoms
>   *Large broken hand mirror

ROD OF BLAME - A large straight metal rod (for instance a fireplace poker)

BUSH OF BITTERNESS - Large, prickly-looking bush

ARMOR - 2 sheets of tin foil, approximately 10" x 10" – one to cover a fresh orange in bowl behind Lisa; the other for when Satan covers her mangled heart/orange

BUSYNESS - Large cordless stereo headphones, visible earbuds, or shop earmuffs

KLEENEX – For audience afterward

The SET can be extremely simple or elaborate, depending on your resources, building, and unique situation. Some groups have even done this as a street ministry with only a stool and piano bench. Others have performed this play on a stage with a couch, bed, or mat for LISA to lay on when crying, and other furniture. It's all up to you and your creative imagination and needs.

MUSIC SUGGESTIONS BY SCENE

[When several ideas are listed, only choose one. Feel free to add your own, updated music. While most churches have a license from CCLI for Christian music, you may need to obtain a master license from the record label that owns a secular recording, and possibly a performance license from the publisher that controls the song composition to use popular music.

Some groups have used live musicians effectively. For help with obtaining licensing, please consider using the services of Easy Song: https://www.easysong.com/services/licensing/get-permission/custom/ *They have resources that will save you a lot of time and effort. On the other hand, if you decide to use original music, please make sure the song truly fits the scene.]*

Scene 1 Music Ideas:

"I Still Haven't Found What I'm Looking For," by U-2
"Longer," by Dan Fogelberg
"I Want to Know What Love is," by Foreigner

Scene 3 Music Ideas (beginning):

"This Ain't Living," by G. Love and Special Sauce

Scene 3 Music Ideas (end):

"Love Hurts," (permission to use this song granted by
Boudleaux Bryant, House of Bryant). Option: version by Joan
Jett, on her "Joan Jett—The Hit List" CD
"Latter Days" by Over the Rhine, from their *Good Dog Bad
Dog* CD
"Do You Really Want to Hurt Me?" by Culture Club
"Unbreak My Heart," by Toni Braxton
"Brokenhearted Girl," Beyonce
"Song for the Broken Hearted," by Lee Carr

Scene 5 Music Ideas

"Take a Look Around: MI 2 Theme" Limp Bizkit version, the
angry sounding chorus, "I know why you wanna hate me..."
"Harden My Heart," by Quarterflash
"You Can't Break a Broken Heart," by Voegele

Scene 6 Music Ideas:

Crazy, techno music -- such as instrumental piece from
Mission Impossible 2 sound track

Scene 7 Ideas Music (beginning):

"You Remain," by Jennifer Knapp
"He Knows," by Jeremy Camp

Scene 7 Ideas Music (at the end):

"Broken Things," by The Williams Brothers, on their
Harmony Hotel CD (My personal favorite)
"The Nails in Your Hands," by Seized by the Power on their
Everybody Duck CD
"How Could You Say No," by Billy Sprague
"Hiding Place," by Sara Groves
"By Your Side," by Tenth Avenue North
"Broken Vessels," by Hillsong
"Beautifully Broken," by Plumb
"Whole Heart (Hold Me Now)," Hillsong United, (church
online version, not the live version)
"Mended," by Matthew West
"Perfectly Loved" by Rachael Lampa

Many folks have learned that it is effective to follow the conclusion of the play with 30 minutes of soft worship music while people are given time to pray and be prayed with by leaders and/or cast. *[See Post-Performance Suggestions instructions on page 50.]*

SCENE 1

*(Stage is **dark**. Play **opening song**. As the song is played, the **lights rise to low** revealing a girl, LISA SMITH, wearing pigtails, and sitting on a tall stool or piano bench with an orange on her lap, C stage. She is frozen with her head bowed. SATAN is off stage UR and JESUS is off stage UL. **As the song gradually fades**, the **lights go on full** when the NARRATOR begins to speak and LISA and MRS. SMITH both come to life. MRS. SMITH enters UR as song is playing, looks wistfully at LISA who is making mud pies and smiling with childlike innocence. LISA is in a happy-go-lucky mood, pretending to play with her mud pies. MRS. SMITH is distraught, trying to figure out how she is going to break the sad news to LISA.)*

NARRATOR:

Meet Lisa Smith. She is a happy, healthy, five-year-old girl. Her favorite pastimes are helping Mom in the kitchen, playing with her play dough or mud pies, visiting grandma on Sundays and going to preschool two days a week. A full and exciting life, with lots of love and security. But then one day...things change.

MRS. SMITH: *(nervously)* Lisa, I have something to tell you.

1

LISA: *(in a child's voice)* Oh hi, Mommy. I have something to tell you, too. I just made a mud pie, but it doesn't taste very good.

MRS. SMITH: *(disinterested)* Oh, that's nice dear. *(Puts her hand on Lisa's shoulder and sits beside Lisa on the bench)* Honey, I have something important to tell you. I know that this will be hard for you to understand right now *(pause)*, but... Daddy and I are getting a divorce.

LISA: *(puzzled)* Divorce? What's a divorce?

MRS. SMITH: Well, it means that Daddy and I won't be living in the same house anymore, and...

LISA: *(interrupts, upset)* What?

MRS. SMITH: Now honey, you want Daddy and me to be happy, don't you?

LISA: Yes, but...

MRS. SMITH: And you know we aren't happy when we fight all the time. We just don't love each other anymore, so he's going to move away. It will be better this way.

LISA: *(emotionally)* But no! That can't be! No, Mommy!

MRS. SMITH: *(controlled)* Please don't worry. It's going to be okay. You can visit Daddy one weekend a month and he'll even take you to the zoo... that's your favorite place to go. It's going to be okay, I promise. It's going to be okay. *(Exits UR.)*

(LISA pauses with orange in hands as her emotions come to the surface, she stands and walks DL.)

LISA: It's not fair! Daddy... Daddy don't you love me any more? You must not, otherwise you wouldn't leave. Did I do something wrong?

LISA: *(Moves DR)* Mommy, you must not love me, either, otherwise you wouldn't send Daddy away.

LISA: *(LISA, upset, returns to Center)* I feel like a piece of my heart has been torn away!

(She tears away a piece of the orange and throws it to the ground, sits down in a huff.)

LISA: It's just not fair! *(tearfully)* What am I gonna do?

(SATAN enters and gazes at LISA for a few moments then steps behind LISA'S R shoulder. In all scenes, he is never in

LISA'S full view. He remains sneaky and as though speaking into her thoughts.)

SATAN: Psst! Hey Lisa! Lisa Smith!

LISA: *(looking up and outward)* Who is it?

SATAN: It's me, your friend, Satan. Sounds like
                    something *terrible* has happened to you!
                    Don't worry. I've got just what you need.

(SATAN instantly drops smile to cast a cold glance upon the TWIG and NAIL props in his hand.)

LISA: *(uncertain)* You do?

SATAN: *(with a sinister smile)* Why, of
                    course! I have some toys, just
                    for you.

LISA: *(cheerfully)* Toys? Oh, I like toys!

SATAN: I thought so. This first one (*holds
                    it up)* is what I call *(deliberate)* the
                    TWIG OF BITTERNESS. Here!

(LISA gingerly reaches out to receive it, and studies it with a puzzled look on her face.)

LISA: *(stumbling)* Bitterness?

SATAN:	Yes, you can use this to protect your heart. It will prick anyone who dares to come near.

(LISA holds up her heart (orange) and pretends to ward off potential attackers with the TWIG.)

LISA:	*(smiling)* Hey, that works great! Got any more toys?

SATAN:	Oh, I've got lots more toys, Lisa. Here's one that I call the NAIL OF ANGER *(hands it to her.)*

(LISA reaches out and receives Nail. Her eyes widen as she feels its sharpness.)

LISA:	Wow, that's sharp! *(shrugs)* But what do I do with it?

SATAN:	If someone tries to hurt you, you can *wound* them with it.

LISA:	*(strikes weakly at imaginary enemies)* Like this?

SATAN:	No, more like this! *(Grabs her hand and helps her "jab" more harshly.)* Exactly!

LISA:	*(wide-eyed)* Wow.

SATAN: This next toy is called JEALOUSY.
(Hands NAIL to her.)

(LISA places ANGER on her lap or in a pocket to receive JEALOUSY, inspects it).

LISA: What's this one for?

SATAN: Do you know the little girl down the street who has that pretty red wagon?

LISA: Yeah?

SATAN: *(loudly)* It's not fair that she has one and you don't.

LISA: *(sits up defiantly and gets new nail ready for action)* Yeah!

SATAN: *(very loudly and firm)* She shouldn't have it. *You* should!

LISA: *(stands with determination and walks DR stabbing with the NAIL)* You're right. I want it! Give it to me! It's *mine!*

SATAN: *(nods in approval and triumph)* Very good, Lisa. That's the idea.

LISA: Oooo. I like that one! *(smiling fiendishly as she sits back down.)*

SATAN: And here's one more. It's one of my favorites—ILLICIT SEX.

(After LISA takes the NAIL, SATAN'S smile turns cold for a brief moment.)

LISA: *(innocently)* Sex? What's sex?

SATAN: Oh, you don't know about that now. But when you get older, you'll find out. And when you do, *(boastfully)* you'll thank me!

*(SATAN fades back to UR stage with a fixed, cold expression on his face. LISA shrugs. **Lights fade to medium.**)*

SCENE 2

*(With the **lights still at medium**, the narrator speaks while LISA is on stage playing with her "toys. Light instrumental background **music**.)*

NARRATOR:

Later, we find Lisa in early grade school playing with her "toys". Her mother is exasperated because she cannot seem to control her. She becomes more inconsistent with Lisa's discipline, which, in turn, creates even greater insecurity in the little girl's heart. In spite of Lisa's reaching out for love from her classmates, she has a difficult time communicating with them because they don't like the "toys" she is using. So the grooves of rejection continue to grow deeper as they repeat themselves like a broken record.

*(Stage **Lights rise to full light**. LISA walks DL and smilingly reaches out her HEART (orange) to imaginary friends)*

LISA: Will you love me? *(Pause, then in horrified tone.)* What do you mean, I'm ugly! *(Hatefully jabs with NAIL OF ANGER.)* Well your nose is longer than a garden hose!

LISA: *(Sweetly toward another girl)* Will you be my friend? Let's go play!

LISA: *(Pause. Defensively)* So what if I don't have a daddy around! At least he's not a *fatso* like yours is!

LISA: Won't somebody love me? *(Sits dejectedly on bench.)*

JESUS: *(enters from off stage UR and walks up behind the bench, saying warmly)* Lisa, I love you.

LISA: *(clutching heart)* Who are you?

JESUS: I'm Jesus, your creator. *(Steps beside the bench.)* I want to be your friend and take special care of your heart. *(glancing at her toys)* I want to free you from those things you call toys. They're only hurting you. Will you give them to me?

(LISA shifts, defensively holding her heart away from him.)

LISA: No! I won't give you my toys! They're all I have to comfort me. Go away! *(turns away)* I like my toys.

*(JESUS slowly backs up to UC stage, respectful of her wishes. **Spotlight** on JESUS **fades** and then he returns to UC stage.)*

SATAN: *(approaches UL)* Hey, Lisa! It's me, your friend again.

LISA: *(delightedly)* Oh, hi!

9

SATAN: I saw what your classmates did to you. What
           you need are some more toys.

(SATAN pulls out the NEGATIVE GLASSES which are
hidden behind his back tucked in his waistband or pocket,
and puts them on himself as he talks, looking smug.)

SATAN: You know how people have told you this
           world is a wonderful place to live? That
           everybody loves one another?

LISA: (agrees happily) Yeah.

SATAN: Well, they've *lied* to you, Lisa. (Lisa quickly
           drops smile) It's simply not true.

LISA: (shocked, slumps down) It's not?

SATAN: Of course, not. What you need are these—
           Negative Glasses (whips GLASSES off his face
           and places them on her).

SATAN: They'll give you a whole new perspective on
           life. Then you can see things as they really are.

LISA: (sour look on her face) Ewe. Everything's green!
           Yucky, mossy green.

SATAN: Yep!

LISA: *(looking upwards)* The sky is green; *(looking out at the audience)* People are green; *(looks at herself and is surprised)* I'm green! *(sadly)* I'm yucky.

SATAN: That's right! That's the way it is and that's the way it's always gonna be.

LISA: *(pouty)* Yuck!

(SATAN kneels by the bench on the left and pulls out the ROD OF BLAME lying beside it.)

SATAN: I've got something else for you. It's what I call the ROD OF BLAME. *(Hands ROD to her. LISA stares at it in wonderment.)*

SATAN: You know how your teacher says, "Lisa's such a naughty little girl?" And how your mother gets mad at you for the way you misbehave around the relatives?

LISA: *(abashedly hunching down)* Yeah.

SATAN: *(stands and paces behind her louder and more emphatic)* And your friends, Lisa, how they've let you down? You've got to realize, it's not your fault!

LISA: *(surprised, sitting up)* It's not?

11

SATAN: Don't be ridiculous! They're the ones to blame!
For one thing, your teacher hasn't been fair!
And your mom—*she's* the one who got the
divorce. No wonder you have tantrums! *(Pauses
for effect.)*

SATAN: *(continues)* And your friends, Lisa. They've been
so *mean* to you. It's only natural for you to get
mad at them. Quit blaming yourself. Blame
them! You will feel much better placing blame
where blame is due. *(Slinks backward UR)* Just
remember, it's not your fault. It's just not your
fault! *(Exits UR.)*

*(During Satan's speech, Lisa clutches the rod and nervously
rotates it in her hands, standing as he says "its not your fault.")*

LISA: *(walks DL and in anger cries thrusting the rod
straight out)* Daddy? Daddy, it's your fault!

*(LISA pauses briefly, walks DR, then makes another thrust
with ROD, sobbing.)*

LISA: Mommy...it's your fault! *(short pause, walks CS)*
World! *(thrusting rod outward, strongly)* It's all
your fault!

*(LISA places the ROD to the right of the bench and walks
DR. While **lights are out** she removes her pigtails/braids
and becomes the older LISA. If possible, have her change or*

peel off some of her child-clothes and reveal more mature clothing, like a teenager.)

SCENE 3

*(**Lights** slowly come up once Lisa is looking older. **Music** gently comes on.)*

NARRATOR:

And so, Lisa enters her high school years, with her vision distorted and the vacuum in her heart growing deeper and deeper. The setting seems right for her first real romance. It is at this point that Mike enters her life.

*(**Music** come up in full, as MIKE stands up in middle of the audience and walks toward stage. LISA plays with her hair. He pauses DL, looks over at LISA, she looks away, they do the looking/flirting thing, he looks back at her, approaches C stage. In the interactions that follow, they frequently interrupt one another to make it realistic. **Music fades.**)*

MIKE: Hi, Lisa.

LISA: *(unsure)* Oh, uh, hi Mike.

MIKE: Hey, I really enjoyed working on that
          History project with you.

LISA: *(shyly)* I did, too. It was...

MIKE: I was wondering if you want to go to the game and the dance with me on Friday?

LISA: *(eagerly)* Really? Uh, sure, that'd be great. *(Mike looks relieved.)*

*(**Music** starts up again and continues. They walk across stage SL, talking quietly. She whispers in his ear. They take a few seconds to look at each other and laugh. They walk across stage SR and she swings her hand back for him to clasp as they walk, she leans back against the wall. He leans in and whispers in her ear. They keep whispering in each other's ears, laugh softly, she turns and pulls on his shirt and they walk towards C stage and sit. They start to talk quietly to themselves and laugh. [The goal is to portray a relationship blossoming over time.] **Music** fades and stops.)*

MIKE: Lisa, I want you to know that these last three months with you have been great and...

LISA: *(biting lip)* Yeah, it's been great for me, too. I...I feel so good when I'm with you.

MIKE: *(closer, sincerely and a bit shyly)* Lisa... I love you.

LISA: *(softly)* I...I love you, too.

MIKE: Can I have your heart?

LISA: *(hesitantly takes a breath)* Will you take care
            of it?

MIKE: Lisa, *(places his hand on her shoulder)* you can
            trust me—especially with your heart *(holds
            hand out).*

*(LISA looks in his eyes and places HEART in his hands. Both
smile and pause.)*

*(MIKE smiles, turns away, stands to the side of the bench to
portray a passage of time, then turns back, thoughtful.)*

MIKE: Lisa, I wonder...we've been dating for a while
            now and, well, when two people are in love,
            there is a way to express it that brings them
            closer than they've ever been before *(pause).* I
            think we both know what that is.

*(LISA stands to the other side of the bench, pulls out the
NAIL, looks down at it, plays with the nail nervously; moves
closer and extends NAIL toward MIKE while MIKE is
talking.)*

LISA: You mean this?

MIKE: *(reaching out for the NAIL)* Only if you're
            OK with it and all. I just think that...

(LISA pulls NAIL away, plays with it in her hands.)

LISA: Uh, I don't know. My mom would *kill* me if she ever found out. She always told me it was *wrong*.

MIKE: *(slightly impatient)* Wrong! How can it be wrong when we love each other so much? *(catches himself and becomes less intense)* It just seems like the next, logical step in our relationship.

LISA: *(hesitantly)* I'm just not sure.

MIKE: *(backing off)* No, hey, if you don't want to, I don't want to—

LISA: *(steps towards him)* I never said that *(pauses)*.

MIKE: *(flustered)* Well...

LISA: *(blushes)* Actually, I've been thinking about it, too. *(She looks at the NAIL and plays with it nervously.)* I just want to be careful, that's all.

MIKE: I know, me too. Sex is a very big deal *(pauses, stepping toward her.)* So ...what do you think?

LISA: I don't know what I *think. (pausing)* But I know how I *feel (steps towards him)*.

MIKE: Lisa—*(steps towards her again, their eyes meet and lock)* I love you.

LISA: *(stepping yet closer to him)* I love you, too.

(Standing hip to hip MIKE places his hand over LISA'S, holding the nail and both of them slowly put NAIL into her heart one time. LISA looks at MIKE again. MIKE slowly hands nail back to LISA they smile shyly at each other and take a step away from each other, make eye-contact again and MIKE reaches for the NAIL. She gives it to him. He puts the Nail into heart two times, with a little more determination, this time remaining a step or two away from LISA.

When he's done, MIKE gives the NAIL back. LISA looks down showing some measure of shame and confusion. They turn away slightly from each other and take another step or two apart.

They pause. This time LISA turns slightly away from MIKE and he walks over to her and touches her arm. She flinches and, without looking at him, hands the nail to him.

MIKE takes the nail, walks down stage, and stabs the heart several times looking at LISA now and then [without overdramatically mutilating it].

LISA stands on the far edge of DL and tugs on her clothing a. rubs her neck in obvious apprehension, indicating increasi distance and shame.)

MIKE: *(looks at her nervously)* Lisa, I need to talk with
         you about something *(pauses, rubs back of his
         neck.)* Remember when you gave me your heart
         a while back?

18

LISA: *(turning to look at him, says quietly)*
Yeah…

MIKE: Well, um, I kinda don't need it anymore. So, here (*hands Lisa her torn, leaking HEART*).

LISA: *(shocked)* What? *(takes a step closer)* You don't want it?

MIKE: No, I'm sorry. This whole relationship thing… It's not what I expected. Things just aren't working out between us. Oh, and here's your toy *(hands nail back)*.

LISA: But you can't do that to….

MIKE: *(interrupting)* Don't get me wrong. I think you're a great girl, but it just isn't the same anymore.

LISA: *(starts to cry and steps closer)* But, Mike, you said you *loved* me.

MIKE: I did.

LISA: *(sobbing, taking steps towards him)*
But Mike…

MIKE: *(impatiently, crosses in front of her to SL)*
Don't ruin it now by getting all emotional.

LISA: *(SR, aghast)* I can't believe this. You said we'd be together *forever*!

MIKE: *(SL, obviously uncomfortable)* Well...I didn't mean *forever*, forever. I meant *(sighs)* I guess I don't know what I meant. I'm sorry, I'm just confused right now. I need some space *(starts to exit)*.

LISA: *(pleading)* Please don't go.

(LISA steps towards him, they bump into each other. The ORANGE falls to the ground; she spins around and ends up SL.)

MIKE: *(backing off to SR)* Look, I just need to be by myself, all right? It's *over (exits)*.

(Heartbreak Music *begins as MIKE leaves. During the music, LISA drops to her knees and scoops up her heart, sobbing. Then she climbs on the bench and sits cross-legged still crying. Looks at the nail in her hand and agonizingly puts it back in her pocket. She stands and goes DL. She finds a blanket which she tosses aside in exasperation. LISA, curls up with a pillow and cries herself to sleep. JESUS enters and covers LISA with the blanket she tossed aside, remaining with his hand on her shoulder for a moment as he gazes at her in concern. Then he returns to his place on UC stage.* **Lights turn low** *and* **music dims.)**

SCENE 4
(Optional scene—added after the original script)

SATAN: Good job Mike! *(Mike hangs head)*. Oh, don't worry about her feelings (*gesturing at LISA*)...or yours for that matter. It felt good, didn't it?

MIKE: Yeah, it felt great at the time.

SATAN: Well, there you go. If it feels good, *(evil tone)* do it. *(back to salesman tone)* Listen to me well, my friend. No one else in this world is going to look out for you. You've got to take care of #1 if you want to get anywhere.

MIKE: But I feel sort of guilty about Lisa.

SATAN: *(flippantly)* Ah, quit feeling guilty and get on with life.

SATAN: *(continues)* Guilt just wastes time and energy. You only go around once, you know. Enjoy yourself.

MIKE: What do you mean?

SATAN: Well, let me put it this way: You can either sit here moping and feeling guilty for the rest of your life, or...

SATAN: *(continues, in a used-car salesman voice while opening briefcase on bench)* For no money down and just a low monthly payment, you can invest in my "Imitation Life" program. *(pulls BACKPACK out of his BAG and begins to help MIKE put it on)* Here. try this on.

MIKE: *Imitation* Life?

SATAN: You bet! You'll be *imitating* what many others have already done. *(Finishes getting BACKPACK on).* Yep, *(pulls straps tight)* one size fits all.

MIKE: *(puzzled)* There's not much to it.

SATAN: Hey, Mikey, you ain't seen nothin' yet.

SATAN: Let me show you just a few of the items included in my program. First of all, and most importantly, "money" *(removes $20 bills from his briefcase, holds them up and gives to Mike.)* Money is the key to everything you want in life.

SATAN: *(continues)* It opens doors for you that nothing else can. Hey, if you don't have money... *(snatching money from Mike's hands)*

SATAN: ...you can't be happy *(places money in backpack)*.

MIKE: That makes sense.

SATAN: Next, we have S-E-X *(pulls out Playboy and slaps it onto Mike's chest. Mike immediately opens as if looking at Centerfold.)* You already know how great that is *(elbows Mike in jest)*. Now you can enjoy it even more - casual sex, steamy sex, cyber sex ...Oh, and uh, *(pulls out string of condoms)* **safe** sex. Enjoy, enjoy, enjoy. *(Folds condoms in magazine, places in BACKPACK.)*

MIKE: *(Raises eyebrows, smiles.)*

SATAN: I think you've got the right idea *(pause.)* The third item I have to offer is IMAGE.

(SATAN pulls a mirror from his bag, looks into it, flashes it so audience can tell what it is. Satan hands it to Mike who looks into it and begins to adjust his hair.)

SATAN: With this you will be the envy of all your friends. All you gotta do is create a certain look. No matter how you feel or what it costs, always *act* like you've got it together. *(Satan jerks mirror back and puts it in BACKPACK.)*

MIKE: Wait 'til the guys see this.

SATAN: Finally, the last item in Phase One of my program is Alcohol and Drugs *(pulls out a bottle of beer and hands it to him. MIKE accepts the beer).*

SATAN: Life is great when you're on a high *(tosses him a bottle of pills.)* Ya got no worries *(Mike seems a little hesitant, holds both bottles awkwardly.)* Come on, your friends are doin' it. Don't be a loser. Join the fun *(puts bottles in MIKE'S BACKPACK).*

MIKE: Uh, I don't know...

SATAN: Mike, this package is the best investment you'll ever make. Trust me. *(Closes BAG)* Oh, and don't worry about paying me now—I'll collect from you later *(exits).*

MIKE: I guess I'm really gonna start living now.

(Mike stoops slightly under the weight of his newly filled back pack, obvious to the audience and himself.)

(JESUS walks up DL, opposite the bench from MIKE.)

JESUS: Mike...Can't you see that your selfishness is weighing you down?

MIKE: What do you mean? This is great!

JESUS: *(moves to CS)* Mike, stop for a minute, and look around. Don't you realize how much you've hurt Lisa, and yourself as well? How do you really feel?

MIKE: *(face and shoulders fall, puts hands in pockets)* I feel like crap. I know I treated her badly; I guess I really hurt her. But, it's like I just couldn't help it.

MIKE: *(getting defensive)* Besides, it was a lot of fun—so don't give me any of your rules. I'm experiencing LIFE!

JESUS: But Mike, I created you to know real life, and this...*(leaning over and lifting the strap of the pack)*...isn't it. This is empty.

MIKE: *(mockingly)* Empty? You could have fooled me.

JESUS: They're dead ends, Mike. I want to have a relationship with you, to come and live inside you. I want to help you develop strong character and healthy relationships.

JESUS: *(continues)* I also want to be your friend... *(pause)* and the Father you never had *(MIKE looks startled)*.

JESUS: Mike, I know what you've been through. *(holding out his hand toward Mike)* Will you entrust your life to me?

MIKE: Sorry *(pauses then begins to turn away)* Can't you see that I'm busy? I don't have time for you right now. I'm having too much fun. Besides, *(looks out at audience)* what would my friends think? Come back when I'm an old man. Right now, I don't want you around.

JESUS: *(shakes his head)* If you only knew. But, it's your choice, Mike. I won't force you. I just hate to see you live such a shallow life when you could experience so much more.

JESUS: Remember, *(pauses for emphasis and reaches out toward MIKE)* I will never stop loving you.

(Their eyes lock for a moment, then MIKE looks down. **Lights out.** *MIKE exits, JESUS returns to UC stage.)*

SCENE 5

(Lights come up gradually as NARRATOR speaks. LISA, still lying with her pillow and blanket DL, begins to awaken, in concert with the brightening lights, crying softly.)

NARRATOR:

Night after night, Lisa cries herself to sleep thinking about her hurt and loneliness. The pain of rejection and feelings of shame seem impossible to escape. Reminders of her broken romance with Mike are everywhere. There seems to be no relief from her anguish. She feels like no one understands. Her heart will never be the same.

(JESUS moves toward LISA with a look of compassion. He looks to right stage and beckons MOM to LISA'S side. MOM tenderly touches LISA on shoulder, but LISA pushes her away. MOM exits sadly, and JESUS backs away).

(SATAN enters carrying THORN BUSH behind his back; pauses CS and gazes at LISA, then suddenly tries to get her attention. Lights come to full when he speaks.)

SATAN: Hey, Lisa!

(LISA awaking, looking depressed, rises and sits on the bench or couch, dejected.)

SATAN: Lisa, Lisa, Lisa. You should have known better. There is no love in this world, only compromise...But that's all right because I've helped a lot of people with your problems.

LISA: *(wiping her sniffles)* You have?

SATAN: Why, of course. All you need is a device to better protect your heart, so this won't happen again.

(LISA looks interested. SATAN kneels near her.)

SATAN: Remember when I first befriended you when you were just a little girl? *(LISA nods.)* And I gave you that TWIG OF BITTERNESS? *(pulls out BUSH)* Why look! *(hands it to her)* It's grown into a full-blown THORN BUSH! *(Satan stands)* Ah, the fruit of my, er, your labor!

LISA: *(receiving BUSH)* But what do I do with it?

SATAN: You put that *(strokes chin)*—MESS *(referring to her HEART)*—right in the middle.

(LISA puts HEART in center of BUSH.)

SATAN: And then no one can ever hurt you!

LISA: That's a great idea! These thorns will keep people away.

(SATAN exits, with a smile of accomplishment. LISA pauses, stands and then begins to use the thorny BUSH to ward off would-be offenders; walks DL.)

LISA: Amanda, why do you go out with him? He's such a jerk! They all are! Get rid of him! *(walks DR.)* *(bitterly)* My Dad is here to pick me up? What dad!? Tell him I'll walk home. *(walks DC, pause, faces forward)*. Hmm. This Bush of Bitterness does a good job guarding my heart. It's so prickly. But I feel so lonely in here. I wish there was a way for me to stay protected and *still* experience love *(sits dejectedly)*. I wish someone would try to love me anyway. Doesn't anybody care?

JESUS: *(approaches LISA. In this scene, He comes across solid and central, while Lisa flits around)* Lisa, I care.

LISA: You do?

JESUS: Yes, I've waited so long for you to give Me an opportunity to pour my love out on you. Will you let Me now?

LISA: *(hesitating)* Yeah, I think so...

(JESUS reaches His hand toward her HEART/ ORANGE in the BUSH.)

LISA: *(LISA screams as JESUS' hand nears her heart)* Ouch! That hurts! *(stands and walks DR)* Those thorns are poking me. Go away! I can't take your love right now. It's too painful! Go away. *(sternly)* Get out of here!

(JESUS initially stays put. **Spotlight** *on JESUS* **fades.** *Then he returns to UC.)*

LISA: Ow, these bitter thorns go *both* ways *(crossing to DC)*. They may keep people out, but when someone does try to love me, they go the other direction and poke me, too *(sits with exasperation)*. What am I gonna do now?

SATAN: *(appears quickly)* I've got you covered. Just what you need.

SATAN: *(flashing sheet of FOIL)* Fresh from my laboratories. It's what I call my "ArmorAll Protection Plan!" Come on, give me your heart.

LISA: *(protesting)* But...

SATAN: *(motioning with hand impatiently)* Come on. *(firmly)* Give it to me!

LISA: *(pulls her HEART out of the BUSH and hands it to SATAN)* Fine!

(SATAN turns his back to her slightly and wraps LISA'S HEART [ORANGE] in FOIL, a cold, sinister look on his face. When fully wrapped, he gives the HEART a quick toss in the air. Then he turns, pastes a grin on his face and holds it out to her.)

SATAN: There! Nothing short of a shotgun blast will get through that one *(slaps foil-covered HEART into her hand)*. My Armor is guaranteed to give you *(deliberately)* the hardest–heart–in–town! *(Exits.)*

LISA: *(fiercely)* And then no one will hurt me again!

(Lights totally out.)

(While lights remain out, *play* **music** *chosen for this scene, such as "Gonna Harden my Heart." The darkness allows LISA to* exchange *her beat-up, foil-wrapped HEART with the NEW foil-wrapped HEART that has been placed in a bowl behind her, out of the audience's view. She places this new foil covered HEART inside the thorn BUSH.)*

SCENE 6

*(**Lights come on gradually** and **music fades** as NARRATOR begins to read.)*

NARRATOR:

It is in this state that Lisa enters her Senior year. However, no one would guess how desperate she is because she covers it up so well in a crowd. But when she is alone, the hurt and feelings of isolation seem to overwhelm her.

LISA: *(comes to life, smiling, stands)* Hey high school's really a blast, *(shrugs)* with a few exceptions like homework and stuff. *(thoughtfully)* But when I'm at home and in my room, I feel so alone... *(sits)* So empty.

(SATAN enters, stands directly behind her, glaring at her.)

LISA: I...I just can't shake this cloud of depression that hangs over me. And the memories. Those awful memories. They keep playing over and over in my head, I can't get away from them. If only there was a way I could hide from it all...

SATAN: *(abruptly)* Lisa! What are you doing?

LISA: *(Jumps, startled.)*

SATAN: You're standing still when there's a whole world *(sweeping his hand)* out there passing you by. I know what the trouble is. You spend far too much time THINKING. There are places to go, things to do, people to meet. What you need is... BUSYNESS!

(SATAN puts BUSYNESS [Headphones] over her ears. Crazy, **techno music,** *starts playing in background. LISA stands and starts nodding, getting into the music.)*

SATAN: *(fast)* You gotta get down and get involved in all kinds of sports, parties, music, school activities, and social media. Stay scheduled "24 /7." And most importantly, never, ever slow down.

*(**Music** gets louder and heavier. SATAN fades back to UR stage.)*

LISA: *(moving with the beat)* That's a great idea. I can go to all the games, hit the parties, text my friends during class, get into school activities every night of the week, and when I'm home, watch TikTok videos, and listen to iTunes all night long. And then...(pauses; **music stops** abruptly).

LISA: *(deliberately and bitterly)* ...then I won't have to think about it all. (**Lights fade to medium.** LISA sits.)

SCENE 7

NARRATOR:

And so, as time goes by, we find Lisa run down from all the activities she's been into, but still with a gnawing dissatisfaction inside. Her "toys" aren't enough, yet she holds onto them because there is no better alternative.

(Lights come up slowly.)

LISA: *(awakening)* These activities have been great, but if I stop for even a moment, I realize I am still empty inside. I wonder if there's more to Life—like God or something. I wonder if He exists. For that matter, I wonder if He knows *I* exist. Even if He did, I doubt He'd care about anyone like me. Especially if He knew everything.

(JESUS slowly approaches, stands behind her, with a warm look on His face. In this scene, again, JESUS comes across as solid, while LISA flits around at times.)

LISA: *(reaching up with emotion)* But if Your love is big enough to reach down and...(stops, sighs, drops hands.) This is ridiculous! I'm better off playing with my toys and *pretending* things are okay than simply talking into thin air!

*(**Music** [such as, "You Remain" by Jennifer Knapp] plays as LISA begins to silently "play" with her toys. JESUS stands behind LISA and puts a protective hand out as she stabs at the air with the NAILS, holds up the BUSH, or stabs with the ROD of BLAME. This action goes back and forth. LISA gets more and more frustrated with her toys and their ineffectiveness as time goes on.)*

LISA: *(sighing)* At times, I get the strangest feeling that someone is trying to talk to me...

JESUS: *(quietly)* Lisa.

LISA: Like God or something.

JESUS: Lisa.

LISA: God, is that you?

JESUS: Here, let me take some of this Busyness from you *(reaches out and removes HEADPHONES from LISA)*. It only keeps you from hearing me.

JESUS: You see—I came to give hearing to the deaf. *(Pauses to allow impact to sink in, then sets headphones down on bench behind LISA)*.

LISA: *(notices JESUS)* Eew! You're green! Who are you?

JESUS: *(smiles)* I'm Jesus, Lisa. Let me remove those glasses from you *(removes GLASSES)*. They distort your vision and keep you from seeing me as I really am.

LISA: *(blinking)* Wow, it's bright out here.

JESUS: That's why I came...to give sight to the blind *(pauses, sets glasses away)*.

(LISA stands up and walks DR.)

JESUS: Lisa, I've been waiting for you your whole life. You are so dear to me. I created you and I long to hold you in my arms and comfort you.

LISA: You do? To comfort me? Really?

JESUS: Yes, Lisa. More than you know. If you had known how precious you are to me, you wouldn't have been so afraid of me.

LISA: But I'm scared you'll ruin my life. My fun.

JESUS: Running your own life has gotten you nowhere. I think it's time you consider giving your life to me.

LISA: *(steps away)* But what will my friends think? They'll think I've gone all-religious on them, or something.

JESUS: I know the feeling. *(LISA looks at Jesus)* They mocked me, made fun of me, and even spit in my face. I know what it feels like to be rejected.

LISA: I just don't want to lose my friends.

JESUS: Your friends may let you down, but I never will. I will always be here for you *(reaches out open-palmed hand)*. Lisa, will you give me your HEART?

LISA: *(looking down at her HEART, tries to hide it)* But it's torn and ugly. I don't even want you to look at it!

JESUS: *(reaches out)* I will accept it the way it is. Trust me.

LISA: Trust you? Don't be ridiculous! *(crosses over in front of JESUS to DL)* Every time I've given my heart away I've been hurt. My parents, my friends, Mike, even Satan. They all betrayed me.

JESUS: *(nods head in understanding way)* I was betrayed, too.

LISA: Well, then, how can you expect me to trust you?

JESUS: Because I *died* for you.

LISA: You died for *me*? Why?

JESUS: Because I love you. There was no other way for you to be free *(continues to extend hand to her)*.

LISA: *(pensively removes HEART from bush)* You love me? You loved me that much? *(lets breath out)* Here.

(LISA slowly hands HEART to JESUS, still wrapped in foil. JESUS smiles, puts HEART away for the moment. LISA steps back suddenly realizing her "toys" are exposed and feels shame over them. She turns slightly away from JESUS as if to hide their ugliness with her body.)

JESUS: Lisa, I want us to be close. But those things you call "toys" will only hurt our relationship. *(LISA backs away.)* Will you give them to me?

LISA: But they're my friends! *(LISA looks at him pleadingly.)*

JESUS: Your friends? How can you say that, Lisa? They've ruined every relationship you've ever had. They are *destroying* you, and you call them your "friends"? You need to give them to me.

JESUS: *(continues)* Why not start with all that BITTERNESS?

LISA: But this Bitterness protects my heart!

JESUS: Protects you? Look at yourself. It's only
          poisoning you.

LISA: *(pauses, looks at BUSH, slumps shoulders)* You're
          right. Here *(slowly hands him the BUSH).*

JESUS: *(lifting the thorny BUSH – he raises it to his
          head)* These are the THORNS that pierced
          my head and stabbed my brow. I took your
          BITTERNESS upon my own head so you
          could be free *(pauses so impact sinks in).*

LISA: *(shocked, turns toward him)* You suffered for
          my BITTERNESS? Oh my gosh! I didn't
          know. Jesus, I'm so sorry for doing that to you.
          Please forgive me.

JESUS: *(kindly)* I forgive you, Lisa *(pause).*

*(LISA pulls NAILS out of her pocket and fondles them.
JESUS reaches out his hand.)*

JESUS: What about the nails?

LISA: *(holds NAILS away from Jesus)* Don't touch
          these!

(LISA catches herself. Looks at JESUS, then at the NAILS with sadness. JESUS keeps his hand ready.)

LISA: I'm sorry. *(Slowly looks at first NAIL as if for one last time)* Here's ANGER. *(Hands over the NAIL with hesitation)* I've hurt a lot of people with it, especially my mom. And *(slowly holds second one out)* -- here's JEALOUSY *(gingerly hands over the NAIL)*. I've wounded a lot of friends with that one.

(LISA hides third NAIL, crosses the stage in front of JESUS to DR.)

JESUS: There's one more.

LISA: *(with emotion)* But Jesus, I can't! I feel so ashamed *(looks down, clutching the NAIL and turns away.)*

JESUS: Lisa, I love you and accept you regardless of what you have done. You don't need to keep this from me. I want to free you from your shame *(holds hand out, waiting).*

(Looking away, LISA hesitantly hands JESUS the last NAIL in the same way she handed it over to Mike.)

JESUS: These things you call "toys"...(*touches her shoulder with one hand to turn her to look at him, while gripping the NAILS with his other fist, arm outstretched as if on the cross*)...are what <u>nailed</u> me to the cross (*pause for effect*).

LISA: (*shocked at sight of his fist of NAILS*) I...I did that to *you*? Oh Jesus, I'm sorry. I was *so* wrong. Please. Please forgive me.

JESUS: (*respectfully pauses*) I do forgive you (*puts NAILS away; pauses*).

(*LISA nervously reaches down and picks up the ROD of BLAME.*)

JESUS: Lisa, I want you to give me the Rod of Blame. It's not good for you to go on like this.

LISA: (*clutching the ROD as she did before*) But Life just hasn't been fair!

JESUS: Lisa...

LISA: (*whips around, pointing the ROD at Jesus' side, angrily*) But it's *your* fault!

(*JESUS pauses; takes the ROD from Lisa and holds it into his side for a second*)

JESUS: This is the spear that pierced my side and broke my heart. I took the BLAME for you so you could be free.

LISA: *(turns toward him)* Oh, Jesus, I blamed everyone else for all of my hurts and disappointments, some of which I did to myself. I even blamed you.

LISA: *(continues)* I never thought I was hurting you. I need you to forgive me.

JESUS: Lisa, I forgive you *(sets ROD down)*. There is one more thing. I need to remove the Armor from your heart, which has hardened you from receiving love.

(JESUS picks up the foil covered HEART, the new one Lisa secretly exchanged in the bowl behind her in the dark at the end of Scene 5.)

LISA: But my heart is such a mess *(crosses over to DL, clutches self in fear of exposure while Jesus unwraps HEART)*. I don't even want you to *look* at it!

(LISA drops her shoulders and turns away, wrapping her arms around herself as if feeling exposed, scared, vulnerable.)

(JESUS fully unwraps foil from new, exchanged HEART.)

JESUS: Lisa, I have a surprise for you *(JESUS gently taps her shoulder and shows her the fresh, clean, unwrapped HEART).*

LISA: *(gasps)* Why...Why...It's healed! It's brand new! *(happily)* I...I don't believe it!

(Both smiling, they stand together CS.)

JESUS: This is why I came...to *heal* the brokenhearted.

LISA: *(happily)* Oh Jesus, how can I ever I thank you?

JESUS: It's like I promised, Lisa. My love is faithful. I will always be here for you.

(Intro to music *[such as "Broken Things"] begins softly)*

JESUS: When anyone comes to me, I will make them a new person. And the old? The old is past and gone. Now everything is new. All I ask is that you continue to trust and follow me so I can keep it this way.

LISA: *(smiling, looks at Jesus)* Jesus, you have given me a new life! I love you.

JESUS: *(also smiling, puts his arm around her for a gentle hug.)* I love you too, Lisa. There are so many things I want to show you...

*(**Music comes on full as the lyrics begin.** JESUS and LISA walk DL for a teachable moment. JESUS appears to be showing or explaining things to LISA about the world, herself, or her heart. Their body language indicates moments of joy as well as moments of instruction. In order to NOT make it look romantic, LISA always looks up to JESUS and he avoids leaning down or into her.*

JESUS and LISA cross and stand DR. Then MIKE enters, wearing his BACKPACK. He beckons to LISA. LISA looks toward him, hesitates, and looks to JESUS. JESUS puts one hand on her shoulder and they both beckon MIKE to join them. MIKE shakes his head and quietly leaves the stage. JESUS comforts LISA. They walk DL for a teachable moment. LISA stands on the center-side of JESUS.

SATAN enters and beckons for LISA to come over to him. LISA steps forward, stops as JESUS places his hand on her shoulder to stop her. JESUS steps around her, between her and SATAN. JESUS will be at center stage at this point. JESUS glares at SATAN and authoritatively motions for him to leave, pointing toward exit. SATAN cowers, scowls, and quietly leaves stage.

MOM enters the scene. JESUS then directs LISA'S attention to her mother who appears apprehensive. LISA turns toward her mother then looks back to JESUS, who nods his head. LISA goes to her mother they embrace. Jesus moves behind the bench. LISA and her mother talk softly for a few moments as if LISA is apologizing. They hug again. As MRS. SMITH leaves the stage,

LISA returns to the bench. JESUS stands directly behind her with his hands on her shoulders. ***Lights soften to "Nativity lighting."*** *JESUS and LISA pan the audience. At the* ***conclusion of the song****, LISA holds up her new HEART, all smiles.* ***Lights out.)***

Post-Performance Suggestions:

Try to avoid an abrupt ending to the play. I've seen the best results when time is allowed for personal prayer afterward, with **soft worship music** in the background, such as a repeat of the **last song**, followed by other **worshipful music**. This allows people who are crying to not feel as self-conscious. Crying or sobbing is not unusual. Be sure to have plenty of Kleenex ready.

Make the room a place where no socializing is allowed. If done at church or a camp, encourage those who prefer to leave, to leave quietly so those who choose to stay are free to ponder or pray.

Have leaders or cast members be available to pray with audience members. A reassuring touch on the shoulder or comforting hug may be all the person needs. Some folks may want to talk to the Lord quietly, under their breath; while others may want to have a helper pray to God on their behalf.

Some camps like to allow for a "cabin time" after kids or adults have been allowed alone time. This can be a special experience as people share what parts of the play meant the most to them.

Try to allow the Holy Spirit to lead. May God richly bless your production!

Group Discussion/Reflection Questions

1. Which character in the play did you most relate to? In what ways?

2. Which "toys" have you used to cope with the hurts or disappointments in your life?

3. What obstacles have kept you from surrendering your whole heart to the Lord?

6. What aspect of the Cross struck you most powerfully?

7. Which "toy" do you feel like the Lord is calling you to surrender to Him?

8. Pray for one another in this regard. (Allow for confession, grief, and tears of repentance.)

9. As you pray for each person, have each person accept forgiveness from the Lord. Then thank Him for that forgiveness.

About the Author

Linda (Medill) MacDonald (AKA Linda J. MacDonald) has worked with youth and adults for many years in various ministry positions. While Linda took drama for two years in junior high, played roles in musicals, and wrote short skits for youth endeavors, she considers *BROKEN HEART* a special, one-time inspiration.

She has a long history of volunteering for Young Life, a ministry near and dear to her heart. When she received the inspiration for the play, she was a Lay Counselor for a local church. Young Life found out about it and passed it along to its camps and churches around the country.

She later went back to college to become a Marriage and Family Therapist, specializing in helping folks recover from infidelity and other causes of broken hearts, for 33 years before she retired in 2021.

In 2010, Linda wrote, *How to Help Your Spouse Heal from Your Affair: A Compact Manual for the Unfaithful*. So far it has sold 112,000 copies in paperback, Kindle, and audio formats. She is currently working on a book for betrayed and abandoned spouses. She has a number of blog posts you might enjoy on her website: www.lindajmacdonald.com/Blog

Linda enjoys home decorating, crafts, hiking, traveling, writing, and discussing theology with her pastor-husband, Dan. They love spending time with each other and with their shared adult children and eight grandkids.

Made in the USA
Middletown, DE
13 November 2022

14825206R00040